You're On!

T0150357

You're On!

101 Tips to improve your public speaking skills

Ruth Stotter

Parkhurst Brothers Publishers

MARION, MICHIGAN

www.parkhurstbrothers.com

Parkhurst Brothers books are distributed to the trade through the Chicago Distribution Center, and may be ordered through Ingram Book Company, Baker & Taylor, Follett Library Resources and other book industry wholesalers. To order from Chicago Distribution Center, phone 1-800-621-2736 or send a fax to 800-621-8476. Copies of this and other Parkhurst Brothers Publishers titles are available to organizations and corporations for purchase in quantity by contacting Special Sales Department at our home office location, listed on our website. Manuscript submission guidelines for this publishing company are available at our website.

Printed in the United States of America
Paperback 978-1-62491-082-1
E-book 978-1-62491-083-8

First Edition, 2016

2016 2017 2018 2019 2020 16 15 14 13 12 11 10 ... 6 ... 2 1

Library of Congress Cataloging-in-Publication Data Pending

Parkhurst Brothers Publishers believes that the free and open exchange of ideas is essential for the maintenance of our freedoms. We support the First Amendment to the United States Constitution and encourage all citizens to study all sides of public policy questions, making up their own minds. Closed minds cost a society dearly.

Cover and interior design by   Linda D. Parkhurst, Ph.D.
Proofread by   T. Percival Lamont
Acquired for Parkhurst Brothers Inc., Publishers by: Ted Parkhurst

092016

For assistance with this manuscript I am greatly indebted to Sharon Jones (Vision International Publishing Company in Mill Valley, California), Barbara Fuller (Editcetera in Berkeley, California), Book designers Andrea DuFlon (Berkeley, California), Lucinda deLorimier (Grass Valley, California), and Linda D. Parkhurst (Marion, MI). For assistance with my public speaking skills, I thank Betsy Blakeslee and Verna Winters, both of Berkeley, California.

This is also an opportunity to express my appreciation to my family, Lawrence, Daniel, Jennifer and Steve, for their many generous years of playing audience— providing feed-back and support.

Your spirit of humility, balanced with your entertainment are as important as the content of your talk. Your audience cannot have a good time if you are in agony or if you do not sound interested in what you are saying. Help them by having fun while sharing your expertise.

Keep in mind that if you are trying to persuade your audience to adopt or change a belief this is directly related to their liking and trusting you. Remember, your audience wants to like you and your speech or story.

Contents

Obatala, Lord of the universe, decided to test the wisdom of Orulu, and ordered him to prepare the finest food he could think of, so Orulu prepared ox tongue. When Obatala asked, "Why is this the finest food?" Orulu answered, "What can be more important than the tongue? With the tongue we teach good manners and virtue, we talk of great matters, and praise those who are deserving."

The next day Obatala said to Orulu, "Today I want you to fix the worst food that you can think of."

Again, Orulu prepared ox tongue, Obatala was shocked. "Orulu, how is it possible for the best to also be the worst?" Orulu answered, "I told you that the tongue is the best, but it can also be the worst. The tongue can slander, destroy good reputations, and ruin whole nations." Obatala marveled at Orulu's wisdom.

—Adapted from a Cuban tale reported by Ramon Guirar

CHAPTER 1

How to Begin

Make a folder in which to keep the following information about your event:

— The name, e-mail address, and phone number of your contact person

— Map, GPS address, or directions to the place where you will be speaking and the telephone number at that location

— The scheduled time for your talk to begin

— The allotted time for your talk

— Your contract (if you have one)

— A description of what you will wear, as you do not want to be stressed on the day of your talk with selecting clean, comfortable, and attractive clothing. (Also note if you will be wearing a lavaliere microphone (see TIP 80)

2

Make a list answering the following questions:

— Why are you making this talk?

— Who is your audience?

— Why were you asked?

— What points do you hope to make?

— What obstacles do you foresee in accomplishing your goals?

— If you hope to persuade people to change their opinions or to see an event or issue from a different perspective, what preconceived ideas might people have?

Be honest as you list your ideas, feelings, and thoughts. For example, if you are new in the community and hope to make a good impression, new friends, or network in your career, put these things on your list. Above all, you want to demonstrate sensitivity to your audience, as well as provide relevant facts and a satisfying listener experience.

3

Put these lists away for at least one day. Then review, adding new ideas and thoughts. By answering these questions in writing, rather than just thinking about them, you have already begun the speech writing or storytelling process.

CHAPTER 2
Writing Your First Draft

As you write your first draft, remember that it is a rough draft. Don't try to make it perfect. It is easier to delete material than to develop new ideas. Write down everything you think might be of interest or applicable. Then prioritize this draft with colored highlighter, using one color to mark items that you feel are most important, another color for lesser important items, and a third for the least important items.

Do your research. Even if you thoroughly know and understand your topic, double check the accuracy of your information and seek out up-to-date facts and quotations. Check the pronunciation of unusual words.

6

If appropriate, incorporate local names, streets, personalities, or other information that link you to the group you are addressing. Humor can be an excellent attention-confirming tool, as a part of your opening.

Example:

A speaker addressing a state poultry organization opened her speech by telling her audience that her grandfather, who lived well into his eighties, had eaten a hard-boiled egg every morning of his life. She said that she received a standing ovation before she even began her talk!

7

Sincerity is persuasive. Don't say anything that you don't believe. Avoid stories or anecdotes that you don't personally enjoy, even if they support your point.

8

As you write your story or talk, remember that you will be "telling" it in oral language. Spoken language does not use the same rules of grammar as written speech. You do not need to always speak in complete sentences. You can repeat a word or phrase for emphasis, for poetics, for humor, or to build tension.

Example: Barbara always wore purple. Purple blazers. Purple hats. Even purple shoes. Sometimes, bright purple. Sometimes, soft lavender. From head to toe— purple. She was known as the "purple lady."

CHAPTER 3
Creating A Speaker's File

9

As you revise your story or speech, save the ideas, stories, and quotes that you have eliminated from your earlier drafts. These items may be exactly what you need for another time. Store these in your *Speaker's File* folder.

Other ideas to keep in your Speaker's File:

10

~ Whenever you see a joke, cartoon, or story— whether in print or online—that you think has possibilities for a future talk, cut it out and add it to your Speaker's File.

— When you hear an interesting anecdote or story, add this to your file—with the source's name, date, and contact information. If it is someone else's story or idea, ask for permission to use it and if possible, assure the person that you will identify the source of the anecdote—unless the person prefers that you do not do this. Then be sure to honor your agreement.

— A list of outrageous and/or courageous things that you, a mentor or others, have done or experienced.

— A list of things that terrify you. (After reading this book, I hope you will not include public speaking!)

— Add interesting places you have visited, favorite teachers, least favorite teachers, disappointments or successes, people you will always remember, people you wish you had never met.

These lists are fodder to enrich your talks and stories.

CHAPTER 4

Incorporating Stories and Anecdotes into Your Talk

You will find that people listen to stories, jokes and anecdotes differently than they do to ordinary text. Try it and see! As you begin an anecdote or story, watch your audience shift forward in their seats and their faces assume an expectant quality.

Two Sides to An Argument

Two farmers who were always arguing, were working in their fields on opposite sides of the road when a stranger walked down the road wearing a very attractive hat. "My," said the first farmer, "that was a handsome blue hat."

"Blue!" the other farmer said. "Are you colorblind? That hat was red."

"Don't be silly. It was blue. I saw it."

"Why are you so stupid? It was red."

Just as they were ready to come to blows, the man came back from the opposite direction. This time the first farmer saw that it was a red hat and the second farmer saw that it was a blue hat. Then they realized that the hat was red on one side and blue on the other.

—West African tale (adapted). Collected by Francis and Melville Herskovits. *Dahomean Narrative.* Northwestern University Press, 1958.

The Donkey

A traveler hired a donkey and driver to take him to the next town. When they stopped to rest, the sun was beating down and the traveler sat in the donkey's shadow, where there was room for only one person. "Get up. I want to sit there," said the donkey's owner. "You hired the donkey and not the shadow." "Nonsense," replied the traveler. "When I hired the donkey that included the shadow." While the two men were arguing, the donkey ran off.

Moral: In quarreling about the shadow we often lose the substance.

—*Aesop's Fable*

12

To turn an anecdote into a story, add at least two of the following items:

— Interesting characters

— Dialogue

— Humor

— Suspense

— An opening hook

— A satisfactory closing

Example:

Anecdote: Two men asked a camel whether it was easier to carry a load up or down a sand dune. The camel told them that it didn't matter whether he goes up or down a dune. What makes it easier or harder is the load he has to carry on his back.

Story: Rashid and Ibraham were always arguing. "Your wife makes all the decisions." "You never bring your wife any presents." [Add descriptions. Give the men personalities.] One day they were arguing about whether it is easier to walk up or down a sand dune. [Perhaps they begin this discussion in a tea house and continue it when they meet in the desert.] "You can see where you are going when you go down the hill. "But it is hard on the knees." [Provide a series of arguments to support each man's position.] Finally, at an oasis, they decided to ask a camel his opinion. "It doesn't matter whether I go up or down," the camel told them. "What makes the difference—how easy or difficult it is—is the weight of the load I am carrying."

See Chapter Thirty-Three for a list of books containing short tales useful for speech writers and storytellers.

CHAPTER 5

Revising Your First Draft

13

Re-write your draft using your color highlighters again, this time to organize the main points. Assign a different color to each of your topics and use this color to identify all the information related to that topic. Redo your draft, putting all related material (same color) together. Eliminate all tangential material, even if you like the content or the way it is expressed, saving it in your Speaker's File. Then rearrange the text you are retaining so that it advances and promotes your main points.

14

You don't have to relay an experience in chronological order. You might want to use *"In medias rex"*—Greek for "in the king's reign." This is a sequencing where you start in the middle of the narrative and then go back to fill in the background.

Example: In describing a football game, you may begin with the half-time score, or, begin with the final score.

15

For variation, consider using some of the following techniques:

~ *Change the point of view:* Tell about an event from the point of view of another person or even of an object.

Example: Instead of telling how proud you were to find your first published book on a library shelf in your hometown, try giving the book's point-of-view as it recognizes you.

~ *Allusion:* Refer to something in history or literature. Do not assume that people are familiar with seemingly well-known biblical or historical characters, famous novelists, or movies. Your audience must understand the allusion for it to be effective. You may have to add identifying information.

Example: I felt like Odysseus. You recall the long journey of the Greek King with all of his delays, challenges, and stopovers. Like him, I set out to find my faith.

~ *Metaphor:* Use a word or concept that gives fresh insight into another word or concept, a linkage or association of two different things that shed light on each other.

Examples: "velvet night." "Her smile was the rising sun."

~ *Simile:* Make an object easy to recognize by a comparison using "like" or "as."

Example: She packed her suitcase like a bird building a nest.

A traveler sought refuge on a cold night with a Satyr. He blew on his fingers, and when the Satyr asked why he did this, he explained, "To warm them up." Then, after being served a piping hot bowl of porridge, he blew on his fingers again. When the Satyr asked why he did this, he explained, "To cool them off." The Satyr threw him out, as he would have nothing to do with a man who could blow hot and cold with the same breath.

—A paradoxical tale from *Aesop's Fables*

~ *Paradox:* State an apparent contradiction that is nevertheless true. The shock value accentuates the truth.

Example: A candle lights others and consumes itself.

~ *Irony:* Saying the opposite of what is meant so that there is humor in the incongruity. Use irony carefully, as many people automatically accept what you say at face value. Irony is often fused with satire or sarcasm.

Example: After months of studying for the spelling bee, John lost by misspelling "propaedeutic"—which means preparatory study.

~ *Imagery:* Words that convey the smell, sound, feel, and appearance of people, places, and emotions. Language that appeals to the senses, words that are descriptive and trigger visual images, "painting" pictures in the listener's minds. Help your audience see the dog, or the automobile, or the living room. Verbs can also have visual interest. Instead of "walked," perhaps you could say "tottered," "trudged," "ambled," "stumbled," "jogged," or "marched." If you are describing a color, like a red car or blue shirt, it helps to tie in the color with something the audience is familiar with to help them see the color in their mind's eye.

Example:

Frank, like every male in the firm, always wore a white shirt to the office. This was 1955. Then one day, Frank appeared in a blue shirt. Not pale blue like the sky. No, his shirt was a deep rich blue—like the deep blue of the sea. There was a lot of teasing. However, within one year all the architects in the office were wearing similar deep blue colored shirts. Then, striped shirts, yellow shirts, even purple shirts. White shirts became a rarity. Frank, single-handedly, had started a revolution!

~ *Onomatopoeia:* Words that sound like their meaning.

Examples: Pitter-patter. Tick-tock.

27

~ *Alliteration:* Words that begin with the same sound.

Example: He saw six swans soaring over the sea.

~ *Assonance:* Repetition of the vowel sound.

Example: "Oh, it was so cold."

16

Play with words, sentence construction, and alternative ways to express emotions. Look for words to help your audience feel what you are communicating.

Example:

When the wedding march started, I linked arms with my father and froze. I could not will my legs to move. Terrified, I stood there thinking, "Perhaps this entire wedding ceremony is a gigantic mistake. I don't want to get married. How can I get out of this?" My father started walking and since our arms were linked, awkwardly, I stumbled along beside him. Then something happened. I glanced to the side and saw faces smiling at me. I saw Larry at the altar looking at me,

his eyes shining. I took a deep breath, stood
tall, and it was as if I levitated. I floated
down that long aisle.

AVOID: Marilyn Monroe was a star. She had beauty.
She had talent. She had sex appeal. She had a little girl's
appeal. She had a woman's charm.

INSTEAD: Marilyn Monroe had all the qualities for
stardom: beauty, talent, sex appeal, presence, a little
girl's appeal, and a woman's charm.

17

Keep in mind that you don't have to "say" everything.
What you leave out can be a dramatic part of your talk.

Example: My mother had two daughters. The younger
one she LOVED!

18

Remember to include a thank you to the organization
and/or people who invited you to speak.

CHAPTER 6

The First Three Minutes

Audiences tend to remember the first and last three minutes of a speech or story. Like a person fishing, you want to "hook" the attention of your audience with your opening. This is why many speakers start with, "A funny thing happened on my way here today." However, if your story does not tie in with your topic, if you are not a talented joke teller, or if what you say is not very funny, a joke may be distracting or appear gimmicky. A dramatic opening line or anecdote may be safer.

For a speech entitled
"Wise Investing for the Single Woman"

When I was in the tenth grade, I lost $10,000 in the stock market. Our economics teacher had given us the assignment of investing $25,000 at the beginning of the semester, and at the end of the semester I had only $15,000 of this imaginary investment left. The teacher pointed out that if I had left my money in the first stocks I had picked, instead of buying and selling all semester, I would have been ahead by $7,000. I have never forgotten that lesson.

For a speech entitled "Starting a Mail-Order Business"

Do you get as much junk mail as I do? Magazines that I am not interested in. Catalogs. Pleas from charities I have never heard of. My name is often spelled wrong. Stoffer. Statter. Storrer. Like you, I usually throw these envelopes away, unopened. So why in the world would I, or anyone else, for that matter, think anyone would open another unsolicited mail-order solicitation? Even if your product is exactly what a person wants and needs, your first challenge is to get the recipient to open your envelope. So, let's begin by talking about "The Irresistible Envelope."

20

A sentence or two of "warm-up" introductory material is useful. During your opening remarks, the audience adjusts to your speaking style and your personality. Plunging right into essential information that you want your audience to remember might be a mistake. If they do not know you, they may be distracted by extraneous thoughts. For example, someone might be thinking, "I wonder if her hair is really that color?"

CHAPTER 7

How To End Your Talk

21

Audiences will appreciate your helping them to remember your main points. Near the end of your talk, summarize these, and perhaps provide a mnemonic device.

 Example: So that's it. WHAM. "W" for Wonder. "H" for Heart. "A" for Adventure. "M" for Meditation. The four points I hope you will remember. Wonder, heart, adventure and meditation—the four ingredients I recommend for psychological well-being.

22

Don't be tempted to continue talking after the hit,
the logical place to end your speech or story. Strive for
a crisp wrap-up, not an overly extended wind down.
Construct your closing so that your audience leaves with
a satisfied feeling, or, as the old saying goes, "Leave
them wanting more."

> Two monks, traveling after a rainstorm,
> saw a young woman in a beautiful kimono
> hesitating to cross a muddy road. The
> younger monk picked her up and carried
> her to the other side. Later that evening, he
> older monk chastised him. "You know that
> we are to have nothing to do with women.
> Yet you picked up that woman, and carried
> her in your arms across the street."
>
> "That is true," the younger monk answered.
> "I picked her up, carried her across the road
> and put her down. But you, it seems, are
> still carrying her."

CHAPTER 8
Rehearsing

When you have completed your final draft, get out your highlighters again. Now your speech or story is ready to become your script.

— Use one color to underline dialogue that you will say as if you are talking. Use another color to identify other people's dialogue.

— Use a different color to underline the words you want to say with special emphasis or inflection.

— Mark the ends of some sentences with an upswing, so that you will not end every sentence with lowered pitch or volume.

— Mark places where you will pause. Use a single slash (/) for a short pause, a double slash for a longer pause, and three slashes for even longer pauses.

~ Mark places where you want to use special vocal techniques, such as a whisper or a sound effect.

24

Diagram your talk by making a graph of your key sections to see if the overall structure of your speech or story builds up to an engaging conclusion. Mark points of excitement, emotion, or crisis.

Diagram one shows a talk that initially gripped the audience's attention, leveled out to a plateau, and the interesting material lagged at the conclusion. This is not an interesting format.

Diagram One

Diagram Two shows a talk that peaked too soon, or could have ended earlier.

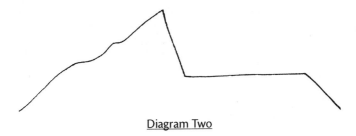

Diagram Two

Diagram Three shows an outline of a more engaging structure. Notice how each section builds to a slightly higher point of interest, and then ends quickly after the high peak has been reached.

Diagram Three

25

Rehearse out loud. As you rehearse, take time to rewrite and revise, converting your written speech or story for an oral delivery. Continue to look for ways to improve your organization and delivery.

Reading your presentation out loud one time equals a dozen silent readings in helping you to remember what is written. Many people find that reading their talk just before going to sleep helps them to memorize it. Consider audio or video recording your work and then listening to it objectively.

26

If you plan to use notes, then make a commitment not to read your entire talk. Find places in your speech or story where you can talk directly to your audience without looking down at your notes.

27

As you rehearse, if you realize that you have forgotten something, just continue with the speech or story. Afterward, reread the section that you left out. Sometimes you will find that what you left out was not necessary and your talk flows better without it. If you do decide to stop and look it up, go back and start the whole thing from the beginning. Otherwise, you will tend to get "stuck" at the same place every time.

28

You can create vocal variety and build interest by varying your vocal intensity and/or inflection when using similar adjectives or adverbs. This is called the three-word build-up. Note that if the delivery is the same for each of these words, they become redundant and you would be better off selecting one word.

Examples:

"John was happy ... excited ... THRILLED!"

"She ran faster and faster and FASTER."

Lowering the pitch:

"I was LONELY ... sad ... depressed"

The three-sentence build-up operates in the same manner:

Examples:

I was hurt. I was angry. I WAS FURIOUS.

My friend woke up on that small island in Fiji to find that his camera had disappeared. His clothes were missing. His food was gone. EVERYTHING HAD BEEN TAKEN.

29

If your talk includes a list of ideas, objects, or people's names or places, be careful not to say these in a monotone pitch or rhythm, as if you were reading a shopping list. A technique actors use to make a list come alive is to envision or feel something different as they say each item.

Exercise:

Read the following sentence out loud, listening to the monotonous quality of reading a list. Then try adding excitement with the suggested emotional or visual associations.

One summer we rented a van and the whole family visited France, Italy, Germany, Spain, Norway and Switzerland.

One summer we rented a van and the whole family visited France (*think of escargot*); Italy, (*think of antipasto*); Spain (*think of paella*); and Switzerland (*think of fondue*); Germany (*think of bratwurst*).

One summer we rented a van and the whole family visited France (*think of your mother*); Italy (*think of your father*); Germany, (*think of a teacher you had*); Spain (*think of a good friend*) and Switzerland (*think of a pet you had*).

41

30

Take time to play with your text as you rehearse. This is a way to loosen you up, to get you excited about your material, to enhance your delivery. As a rehearsal exercise, you might try singing parts of your talk, drawing pictures of key scenes, or even dancing it.

31

When you rehearse, wear the same shoes that you will be wearing when you give your talk. Especially for women, a change in shoe style, as wearing higher heels or cowboy boots, affects your over-all body stance.

32

Rehearse in front of a mirror to observe your facial expression and gestures. Prolong pauses and gestures and see if you like what you see. If you appear bored, you know that you have your work cut out for you. If you are not interested in what you are saying, how can you expect an audience to care about listening to you?

33

As you rehearse, look for places where you can show by gesture or facial expression what is happening.

Example:

Text: He walked by the line of homeless people. They looked dirty and old. He was not going to give them anything. He walked straight ahead into the museum.

Speaker: He walked by the homeless people. [*Mime*

43

a person holding out a cup and begging. Move your hand and eyes from left to right as if someone is walking in front, of you. Then stop and rearrange your body to become the man walking down the street.] He walked on. [*Mime holding your body tight, hands by your side, eyes down, small footsteps in place, angry expression.*]
Then he went into the museum.

When a guru was asked, "What is the secret of life," he answered, "Having good judgment." "I see," said the seeker of wisdom. "And how does one acquire good judgment?" The guru answered, "Through experience," "I see. And how do you obtain this experience?" The guru smiled, "Usually through bad judgment."

34

Schedule rehearsal times. For example, plan to run through your talk at eight a.m., noon, and eight p.m., for three days in a row. It takes discipline to rehearse. Avoid the word practice. You are rehearsing!

CHAPTER 9

Using Repetition

35

Repetition is a valuable technique:

~ To create suspense

~ To build humor

~ To give your listeners time to reflect on a point

~ To provide emphasis

~ To allow time for visualization.

Repetition to build suspense: Her grandmother had told her, "You must never go into the garden." But that night she went into the garden ... into the garden. That night, she went into the garden.

Repetition to create humor: When an action is repeated in your talk, even with disastrous results, the audience will often laugh even before you complete the description.

Laughter will start earlier with each repetition. Repetition as simple as, "She was gorgeous. I mean GORGEOUS! She was gorgeous," can be funny with a humorous delivery. Richard Chase has a character repeat at various points in a story, "I was just studyin' about that," and with each repetition it seems funnier.

Example: Storyteller Donald Davis tells about signing a waiver form to join a group riding mules down into the Grand Canyon. He recited each item on the waiver form as if he were reading it from a contract, for example, "Do you agree not to sue the park service if you are hurt on this expedition?" After each question, Donald wrote in the air a huge, enthusiastic "Y." As each item became more scary —and less plausible—his miming of "Y-E-S" became increasingly frantic and hilarious.

Repetition to give time to reflect, or visualize: He went into the dark forest. He was alone, all alone in the dark forest. He walked, by himself, in the dark forest.

Repetition for emphasis: He said he would never take home any office supplies from his employer. Never. Why, he would sooner strike a child—and heaven knows he would never do that—than steal. He had never, and would never, take anything home from the office. He often told his wife and children, "It is stealing to take even a paper clip home from the office."

CHAPTER 10

Humor

36

Audience laughter is always a delight, and sometimes is surprising when it comes for something you did not realize would provoke laughter. On the other hand, something you think is funny may not receive a laugh. There are many possible explanations. Some people (audiences) just don't laugh out loud. Or, it may be the first humorous utterance, and the audience may not be warmed up or sure if it's okay to laugh. Or, something in your demeanor may not invite laughter. Try to impart a spirit of fun, conveying permission that audible laughter is okay.

37

To arouse laughter, you can tell jokes, use humorous dialogue, describe humorous situations, use sound effects, humorous facial expressions, or set up humor by using foreshadowing. You do not need to try to be a stand-up comic; your goal as a speaker is more complex. Your natural humor, vulnerability, and warmth will provide an intimacy with your audience that is very different than the chemistry sought by most stand-up comics.

Try using some of these types of humor:

~ *Wit* uses the audience's knowledge about a word, idea, or concept, adding a surprise element.

Example: Have you heard about the new book, *Forget about Sex*, by Dr. Ruth Alzheimer?

A convict was playing cards with his jailers, and he cheated. They were so angry with him that they kicked him out of jail.

~ *Pun* uses words that have the same or a similar

sound, but a different meaning.

Example: A king allowed wild animals to roam throughout the kingdom, and the people were afraid to walk in the streets. Then, one day the people abolished the king. That was the first time the "reign" was canceled because of a game.

~ *Sardonic Humor* is self-deprecating.

Example: She'll shop all day for a dress, but do you think she'd put that much effort into looking for a decent man?

~ *Sarcasm* needs a victim. The word sarcasm is derived from "sarkazein"—to tear flesh!

Example: My husband said to me as I walked into the beauty parlor, "I'll say one thing for you darling, you never give up."

~ *Satire* makes fun of society's morals and manners, often with the intent to create positive change. Satire operates like a verbal caricature, often using exaggeration or simplification.

Example: Do you know what Mae West said about having too much of a good thing? "It's wonderful!"

~ *Exaggeration* involves being extreme to the point of absurdity.

Example: It was so quiet we could hear the paint drying.

— *Understatement* also uses absurdity to produce humor.

Example: Once a month Jackie Kennedy went to New York and spent a few pennies on new clothes.

Keep in mind that the first laugh is the hardest to get. Darwin pointed out that there is a series of gradations from a smile to full-blown laughter. This suggests that to obtain laughter, it is a good idea to begin by using slightly humorous material. You may be lucky and have some easy laughers in your audience. Laughter is contagious and one person guffawing often starts an avalanche of laughter.

CHAPTER 11

Suspense

To create suspense, use pauses, repetition, chilling sounds, a hushed tone, or scary character voices. A literary technique is to build to a suspenseful point, then stop and go off in a different direction, leaving everyone curious and anxious to find out what happened.

A man had the same dream every night. In his dream he was exploring a house. Night after night he walked through the rooms, opened doors and windows, counted the stairs and looked in the cabinets. One day, on a visit to a nearby town he saw a house that looked exactly like the house he had been dreaming about. It was the same color, with the same front door and surrounding gardens. He decided to knock on the door and when a woman opened the door he asked,

"Is this house for sale?"

"Oh, yes," she answered,
"but no one will buy it because it is haunted."

"Haunted!" the man exclaimed, "by who?" The
woman suddenly jumped back, her eyes widened,
and as she slammed the door closed, she shouted,
"By you!"

CHAPTER 12

Pause

40

The use of the pause is almost a cliché in speaking manuals for many good reasons.

— A pause can function much like the curtain in a theater, indicating a change in setting, time, or subject.

— An additional advantage of the pause is that it breaks your existing vocal pattern which will help you achieve vocal variety.

— A pause provides time for your audience to visualize the pictures your words are creating.

— The pause is an effective device in building suspense and/or humor.

Keep in mind that the time you pause will seem longer to you than it does to your audience. Try counting slowly to ten in your mind to assure achieving a genuine pause.

Example: "What is it that all women want?" he asked her. (Pause). She smiled, "I will tell you. Come here. (Pause) Come closer." She leaned over and whispered in his ear. "What women all over the world want is …" (Pause)

One way to resist the urge to say "hmmm" or "you know" or "okay" is to pause. Pausing during your talk allows your vocal cords a rest while giving your audience a moment to digest your ideas, images, or argument.

CHAPTER 13

Your Voice

Most people think of vocal variety as using a range of pitch, volume and intonation. Vocal variety can also be achieved through pacing, rhythm, and timing.

— *Pacing:* Tempo (rate of speech). You may start speaking slowly, then pick up your pace as you build to a point, slow down gradually for emphasis, then speed up as you build again to the climax. Try varying your pacing by elongating an occasional vowel.

Example: *I was sooooo scared. Thiiiis is iiit,* I thought!

Another way to vary pacing is by using clipped speech to add drama.

Example: Enunciating carefully, say quickly, "I never want to see you again."

~ *Rhythm:* Word patterns

Example: Empty tin cans and dirty bits of metal.

~ *Timing:* Use of the pause

Example: Pam and Dick were ... talking.

43

If you talk or shout too loudly, it can be unnerving and turn off an audience. Rather than raising your voice, try a loud whisper to achieve the same effect.

44

Strive to enunciate the final consonants at the ends of words. Try it with these words: "Sound—Went—Going" Also, check that you end words with a "z" sound—not "s"—even when the spelled ending is "s"—as in "Doctorz" or "marblez."

45

Avoid saying phrases as if they were written in parentheses. Everything you have chosen to put into your talk should be clearly articulated and readily understandable. Lowering your volume so you become inaudible, or speeding up so that it is hard to catch what you are saying, both indicate this is of lesser importance. If the end of a sentence is said too rapidly, with lowered volume, or without distinct articulation—as often happens with parenthetical commentary—it is distracting, if not inaudible.

46

Avoid using the same voice pattern for each sentence. Some of the patterns that speakers frequently fall into include ending each sentence in a lowered pitch or using pauses of equal length at the end of each sentence. These create a lilting, lulling effect, and you do not want to put your audience to sleep! You can mark your script with a ✓ the end of specific sentences to remind yourself to end these sentences on a vocal upswing in pitch and inflection.

CHAPTER 14
Sound Effects

Sound effects add drama and interest. They also create the impression that you are experienced and at ease. Look for places in your talk to sigh, laugh, cough, use an expression such as "hmmm" or "aha," clap your hands, snap your fingers, click your tongue, or use other sound effects. You might find that using a kazoo, a small drum, or a gong adds drama or emphasis.

CHAPTER 15

Facial Expressions and Body Language

48

Body language: posture, how you balance your weight—even eye-rolls—and your gestures can both enhance or distract from your presentation. If you have a planned movement, such as waving goodbye, or you are going to point to something, do not make these moves quickly. Avoid thrusting your hand out and hurriedly bringing it back to neutral speaking position; this is distracting. Instead, maintain the position of waving or pointing while you deliver the entire sentence. After you point stage left while saying, "The man told me that the school was down the road and to the left," hold your arm extended and keep that gesture for the entire sentence.

49

Look for places where you can make a smooth transition from one gesture into another.

Example: After you point stage left while saying, "The man told me that the school was down the road and to the left," hold your arm extended and keep that gesture for the entire sentence. Then slowly pull your arm back and at the same time bring your other arm forward to mime holding the steering wheel as you say: "And so I continued on down that gravel farm road."

50

Actors use the term "scoring a movement" to help them maintain consistency and believability.

Example:

If you are demonstrating picking apples, decide beforehand exactly where the apples are: how high and how heavy. Remember this choreographed information so that you always put your hands in the same place when you describe picking these apples.

A speaker touching himself or herself while speaking is powerful. However, a gesture unrelated to your talk, such as brushing a strand of hair from your face, is distracting.

Example: Brush your cheek while saying, "It was so soft."

Example: Mime putting on a necklace and patting where it fits around your throat as you talk about a necklace.

52

If you do not know what to do with your hands or arms, know that having them at your sides is perfectly all right. It is important for you to feel as confident as possible while in front of your audience. Therefore, allow your body to follow the content of your presentation. Doing so should result in natural, habitual body movements, which will put your audience at ease.

CHAPTER 16

Special Vocal Techniques

53

Dialogue will make your speech or story more interesting. Look for places to transform description to dialogue. If you have in your text expressions like: "she asked him …" or "her mother told her not to …" or "she wondered …" or "he decided ..." then change the line to dialogue, and deliver it as if that person were talking. You can also use dialogue to shorten long descriptive passages.

Examples: Instead of, "My mother wondered if it would be all right to look in my father's desk," use:

"My mother looked at my father's desk. 'Oh, I want to see if the papers are there, but it is *his* desk. Do I have the right to open his private desk drawer? It may not be the right thing to do, but [pause] nothing ventured, nothing gained. And I need to know.'"

Instead of giving a long description of a living room, use dialogue such as:

We walked into the room. "Look, the little girl said, "there are carved animals on the walls!" Her mother gasped. "I have never seen an Oriental carpet with so many colors and designs. It takes my breath away. This is the most elegant room I have ever seen."

Even if you are describing a personal experience, try to use dialogue. Instead of saying, "I wondered if I would catch that train," use "I was saying, 'Oh, please, don't let the train leave without me. I have to get to Paris for this appointment!'"

54

When you speak in a character's voice, you do not always have to say, "he said," "she answered," or "she replied." In spoken speech, these "speaker tags" add an artificial literary feeling. Eliminating them gives the impression that you are talking to your audience rather than reading a pre-written speech. Change your voice and/or your body stance to identify who is speaking. (See Tip #55.)

Examples:

The girl looked at her puppy. "The house is all neat and tidy now. Now we can eat. Here is your bone. And here is my roll."

ooooo

My boss smiled at me. "Now, Tom, you didn't ask her if she was ..."

ooooo

Mary and Tom were riding into town. Tom was driving.

"Now listen, Mary, I've been there ten years and I've only had one promotion. I am giving notice tomorrow."

"I know, Tom, but Mr. Winters likes you. And besides, the Christmas bonus is next month. At least stay until the first of the year."

Tom clenched the steering wheel. "No, enough is enough. He can keep that promotion money. I have to do this for my self-respect."

"All right, Tom. I understand."

55

If your talk includes a conversation between you and someone else or, between two characters in a story or anecdote, you can establish that a different character is talking by a slight shift of your shoulders. Face the right side of the audience when one character is speaking, looking at them as if they are the character you are addressing. Then shift slightly, to face the left side of the audience as you answer for the second person. Face front as the narrator. You can also change your stance slightly for each character, for example, by hunching up your shoulders to become a character, or bending your knees to show that a different person is speaking. Changing your voice—pitch, rate, nasality—also indicates different characters.

Example:

1. Face front, as narrator: "The church door was open."
2. Shift shoulders and look at the right side of the audience, as character A: "Shall we go in?"
3. Shift shoulders and look at the left side of the audience, as character B: "I'm afraid."

56

When you talk about something you have heard, seen, smelled, or felt, try to invoke that sensory experience. See it in your mind's eye, feel it in your body, summon up the fragrance. Pause to allow your audience time to see, hear, touch, and feel your response. This adds texture and authenticity, making the experience more real to your audience.

57

If you talk about another person, make that person real by adding information that helps the audience visualize and believe in that character. Don't be satisfied with generic labels, "my neighbor," "grandmother," or "little boy."

Example:

Instead of merely saying, "My grandmother always used to say, 'Beauty is as beauty does,'" try this: "My grandmother, with her carefully coiled bun of wiry grey hair held in place with tortoiseshell combs, was fond of using witty sayings and proverbs to make a point. In this case, I think she would have said, in her clear-as-a-bell, emphatic way: 'Remember, child, beauty is as beauty does!'" [Change your posture and voice to become grandmother.] Or …

"My grandmother never left the house without putting on her hat and white gloves. There was always an ironed handkerchief in her handbag. She would sit on the red chintz-covered sofa at night darning grandpa's socks. But as much as she emphasized neatness and cleanliness, she always said, 'Beauty is as beauty does.'"

Many speakers have great success with rhetorical questions. "Can you imagine how I felt?" "Do you know what I did next?" "What would you have done in that situation?" If you use this technique, you do not intend to obtain actual verbal answers. You are just trying to engage the audience's involvement and identification with a situation.

CHAPTER 17

Using Props

59

If you are using a prop with your speech or story, such as a slide show, smart board or white board presentation, video, or backdrop, find someone who is familiar with the equipment and ask them to take charge of it.

60

If you plan to use visual aids, such as Indian baskets or origami flowers—be sure that they are large enough to be easily seen by everyone in the audience. You might prefer to pass your items among audience members, or tell your audience that these props will be on display after your performance.

CHAPTER 18

Getting Feedback—Critiqued

61

Rehearse with a *person.* Welcome feedback. Do not let yourself become defensive. Just listen. Ask your listener to preface commentary with "I." Instead of "You shout a lot," or "You use your hands a lot," a comment might be "I prefer it when you don't raise your voice." "I like it when the gestures complement what you are saying, and I find it distracting when your arms swing as you talk."

You don't want to hear, "That was wonderful!" Well, perhaps you do want to hear that, but you also want to find out what you can do to be even better. Ask the person, "What suggestions do you have?" or, "How can I make it more interesting?" Other questions which will provide useful feedback include:

~ What did you think of my opening?

— Is my talk clearly thought out?

— Does it make sense?

— Could you follow it?

— Did it sound organized?

— Where was it boring?

— How do you feel about the way I ended my talk?

— What did you especially like?

— What did you not especially care for?

— Do you have any comments about my facial expressions or gestures?

— At what point did you get really interested in what I was talking about?

62

Recognize that most audiences want to be entertained and to obtain information, in that order. There is no one right way to give a talk. However, if there is one right thing to do, it is to develop your own speaking style. If you were Mary, participating as one of three speakers at an event, you would not want to overhear audience members saying afterward: "I loved the three talks we heard today. But I can't remember who spoke about roses. Was that Mary or Beth?" Nor would you want to hear, "I loved the way Mary spoke. But what was her topic? Did she talk about roses or ladybugs?"

What you want to hear is: "I loved the way Mary spoke about roses."

A religious man decided he would put his trust in God.

There was a flood, and the officials asked everyone to evacuate. He refused to leave, saying, "God will save me." The waters rose over his doorway, and a fire fighter came with a ladder and asked him to come out. The man declined, saying, "God will look after me." The waters rose, and as he sat on his rooftop, a helicopter came by and lowered a rope ladder. The man waved it away, saying, "God will take care of me." The house was washed away and that night the man bitterly asked God,
"Why didn't you help me?"

"I tried to," God replied, "but you did not listen when I sent the officials, the fire fighter, or the helicopter."

CHAPTER 19

If You Want Audience Participation

If audience participation is part of your presentation style, be sure to practice this with an audience. Decide how you want to elicit participation and to cut it off. Be prepared for unusual responses. Many people do not like to be manipulated into a response, as "Every time I say cat, you say *meow*." Elicit the same effect in an organic way, as "And there I saw a very angry cat. It was saying …" [and lean forward, with one hand cupped to your ear]. Your audience will take the cue. Smile or nod to give positive feedback.

I suggest developing the opening three minutes of your talk after you have the outlined structure of the whole address in place. Your opening can provide foreshadowing—introducing your speaking style as well as your theme

Example: Addressing a conference of children's book authors. Theme: Reality, imagination, and poetic truths.

"How many of you are good liars? [Wait for show of hands] I recommend that those who did not raise their hands to develop this skill. For authors, it is invaluable training. If this scares you, start gently. Try giving a different name at Peets or Starbucks."

Example: Addressing a medical conference for medical professionals. Theme: Looking at hospital experiences from the patient's point of view.

"Wouldn't you be surprised to hear a nurse say as you walked down a hospital corridor, 'I am going to give the medication now to the retired opera singer in room sixteen.' Often the only label we have in the hospital is 'the boy who lost his arm,' or 'the man with cancer.' Patients lose their identity and become labeled as their illness. Not surprisingly, psychologists have found that a label can affect your personality, even your health."

CHAPTER 20

If You Are Being Introduced

64

Most of the time, someone will have volunteered or been assigned to introduce you. Here are some tips for your introduction:

~ You may be asked in advance to provide biographical information for the person doing the introduction. Write out what you consider to be an ideal introduction. Include your interest or connection with this particular topic or audience, as well as your biographical information. Your submission may not be used word for word (introducers like to demonstrate their creativity), but the person assigned this responsibility usually appreciates receiving your material and may use what you have provided.

~ Keep in mind that the introduction both sets you up and is also a useful tool for warming up the audience. You might provide the person who is introducing you with a humorous story about your life, or with other anecdotal information.

~ Do not use the same introduction for all occasions. Prepare your introduction for each particular audience, the occasion, and the purpose of your talk.

~ Omit any self-aggrandizing content that is irrelevant to your topic or the interests of your audience.

~ Ask the person who is introducing you to make any announcements that you would like to have made. For example, your introducer might announce that no video recording, audio recording, or photography will be permitted during your talk. If you have books or other products for sale, ask to have an announcement about where they can be purchased, so that you do not have to push your own wares.

CHAPTER 21

Handouts

65

People like handouts, even something as simple as a bibliography or an outline of your main points. Environmentally conscious people appreciate your using the front and back sides of paper instead of separate pages.

It is possible to hand out something as small as a postcard or bookmark containing your photograph, a slogan or brief biography, and a URL pointing those interested to your website or other online resources.

CHAPTER 22

Home Preparations

66

Checklist of items to bring with you:

- ~ Reading glasses (if you use them)
- ~ A printout of your speech or story
- ~ Handkerchief or Kleenex
- ~ A highlighter and pen in case you decide to do last minute editing
- ~ Business cards or brochures to be displayed, and available for people to take
- ~ Merchandise: books, CDs, videos or audio recordings you are marketing
- ~ Invoice forms or other assets for recording transactions
- ~ Cough drops (Traveling on airplanes and hotel air

conditioning often bring on an itchy throat.)

~ Props (if you are using any)

~ Hand outs

~ Sign-up sheet for your e-mail or mailing list

67

To look your best, a good night's sleep helps! A massage, even the day before, is a wonderful way to help you feel relaxed.

CHAPTER 23
Stage Fright

Some nervousness is good. It shows that you are not arrogant and that you are concerned about doing a good job. It is okay to have butterflies in your stomach. Speaking pros say that "… the secret is to teach the butterflies to fly in formation" (Actress Helen Hayes, 1900-1993).

If you do not know anyone in the group you are speaking to, try to arrive early and talk to a few audience members. Now, you will have some "friends" in the audience. Look for their faces as you speak.

70

Before you begin talking, take a few seconds to look out at the audience and ask yourself, "Do I like this audience?" Look around and search for friends and friendly or familiar faces. "Why, she looks like a nice woman!" "There's Susan!" By doing this exercise, you shift your attitude from being scared and wondering, "Will they like me?" to "Do I like this audience? Why yes, I do."

71

Your attitude has a lot to do with stage fright, as well as with how your audience perceives you. Although you want to be professional and polished, you also want to retain a vulnerability that conveys that you are sincere and a *T* person. Most audiences want double their money's worth—to hear a good talk and to get to know an interesting person. Genuine warmth is a powerful audience connection. Nervousness tends to induce inappropriate smiling, however, and a phony, patronizing, or "please like me" smile, will turn off children and adult audiences alike.

72

If you forget something or lose your place as you are talking, as long as you do not signal your discomfort, your listeners will rarely even notice. If they do notice, they usually don't really care as long as you do not appear distressed. They are there for the content of your speech or story. If what you left out is essential, keep your composure and fill it in a relaxed way.

Examples: If you left out important information:

"Oh, did I tell you that the day this happened was the day before the California earthquake?" Or …

"There is something you need to know. All of this happened the day before the California earthquake."

73

Many speakers create a personal mantra to give them confidence. Repeat your mantra several times the day before, and again just before you begin your talk.

Examples:

"I have a wonderful speech to deliver. They are going to find it very interesting!"

"I am not what is important. The story is more important than me."

"Fun-fun-fun. Both the audience and I are going to have a good time!"

"Just be myself. Be true to myself."

CHAPTER 24

Setting Up Your Performance Space

Arrive early. Check out the physical setting where you will be speaking before the audience arrives. Sometimes a rearrangement of chairs—perhaps with a slight curve instead of in straight rows—creates a friendlier ambiance. If there are distracting posters or furniture, ask that they be moved.

If you are not using a microphone, you still want to arrive early to check the acoustics before you begin your talk. Ask someone to sit in the back of the room and raise their hand if you need to speak louder. Remember, additional bodies in the room will muffle sound.

76

Find the "hot spot" for stage lighting before the audience arrives. Your facial expressions are part of your presentation and it is important that your face be well lit. Talk to the lighting person and find out where the light will be focused and what your parameters of movement are so that you will remain within the circle of light.

The lighting crew at a speaking event I attended had assumed the speakers would be sitting. However, each speaker stood, and as a result, their faces were always in shadow.

77

A dry mouth plagues speakers and affects the speaking voice. Ask the organizers to provide you with a glass of water and that it be placed at an easily accessible height and location.

78

If you are short and will be standing behind a podium, request a wood block on which to stand.

79

Running over your allotted time is inconsiderate. Bring a clock and place it where you can easily see it. Ask someone in the audience to signal when you have two minutes left, and then again when your time is up.

I once attended an event in which the first speaker went over his allowed time by twenty minutes. The second speaker, therefore, had to eliminate half of her prepared presentation.

CHAPTER 25

Using a Microphone

80

Microphones have different qualities. Ask to test the microphone before the audience assembles. Experiment with whispering and other sound effects. Locate the on-off button, and learn how to raise or lower the microphone, and how to remove and replace it on the stand. This is especially important if you are following another speaker. Request that a microphone technician be available to make any necessary adjustments before you begin your talk.

Be aware that a microphone can pick up the sound of jingling earrings and loose pocket change.

Find out ahead of time if you will be using a lavaliere microphone. If so, be sure to dress so that you have a waistband, pocket, or belt on which to hook the battery, and wear a top that allows you to clip the tiny mike clip onto your clothing near your collarbone. If there is a cord connecting these two pieces, it will be hidden beneath your clothing. The advantage of this type of microphone is that you can move around more freely as you speak.

CHAPTER 26
Warm-Ups

Vocal warm-ups are important to help your voice sound relaxed and resonant. Not surprisingly, attitude affects vocal intonation. Smile as you do vocal exercises!

Exercise 1: Put a finger behind each ear lobe and yawn. See if you can feel the opening where the jaw muscles separate at the base of your ear. Tension distorts voice quality. Relax your larynx by saying, "wah-wah-wah," prolonging the "ah" sound.

Exercise 2: Yawn. Push the air out from your diaphragm. Repeat three times.

Exercise 3: Form an "o" with your lips and, starting with low volume, gradually add breath and volume, as you continue to produce the sound. Repeat this with "e," "i," and "ooo."

Exercise 4: Singing helps loosen your articulators—lips and tongue—and open up your resonators—cheek and nose cavities.

82

You are "on" the minute you begin your talk. Many speakers don't appear energized until they are already several minutes into their presentation. A better idea is to find a way to get your adrenalin flowing from the very beginning of your talk. Try these exercises to bring sparkle to your eyes, color to your cheeks, and put you in an "I'm looking forward to giving this talk!" mode.

- ~ Step in place with your right foot and name a fruit. Now step with your left foot and say the first word that you associate with that fruit. Step with your right foot and repeat the last word. Then with your left foot, again say the first word that pops into your mind associated with that word. Then repeat this word as you step down on your right foot.

- ~ Continue this word activity for about three minutes. Have fun! If you do this in front of a mirror, watch your face as it becomes expressive.

You can also do this exercise with a partner. Face each other, and follow the same format. It may go like this:

— First person: Steps on one foot ... "Apple" ... Steps on other foot ... "Red"

— Second person: Steps on one foot ... "Red" ... Steps on other foot ... "Blood"

— First person: Steps on one foot ... "Blood" ... Steps on other foot ... "Doctor"

— Second person: Steps on one foot ... "Doctor" ... Steps on other foot ... "Lawyer"

— First person: Steps on one foot ... "Lawyer" ... Steps on other foot ... "Divorce"

— Second person: Steps on one foot ... "Divorce" ... Steps on other foot ... "Money"

— First person: Steps on one foot ... "Money" ... Steps on other foot ... "Stocks"

83

You want to be centered and confident before and during your talk. While you are waiting to be introduced, close your eyes, listen, and count how many different sounds you can hear. For some mysterious reason, with this simple exercise you will be less likely to be distracted by audience noises (coughing, a baby crying) or outside noises (a train or ambulance).

84

Before you begin your talk, find a place to do physical warm-up exercises.

Exercise 1: Breathing to relax

Take a deep breath through your nose and exhale slowly through your mouth. Repeat three times.

Exercise 2: Head roll for relaxing the throat

Rest your cheek on one shoulder. Slowly bring your head forward and around until it rests on the opposite shoulder. Now, slowly drop your neck backwards and rotate your head, letting it rest on each shoulder

Exercise 3: Take charge exercise to build confidence

Position one: Bend your elbows and extend them out in back as if they were trying to touch each other.

Position two: Keeping your elbows bent, straighten your forearms and swing these behind as if they were trying to touch each other.

Position three: Return to position one

Repeat this exercise ten times

Exercise 4: Arm Swing to energize your body

Position one: Extend your arms in front of you.

Position two: Bending from the waist, swing both arms around to the right as far as they will comfortably reach, moving your upper torso in the same direction. Follow your hands with your eyes

Position three: Return to the first position, arms in front of you, and repeat this movement, to the left.

Repeat in both directions ten times

Exercise 5: The Hawk—Yoga exercise to focus energy

Position one: Place your hands in prayer position in front of your chest

Position two: In this position, slowly push them up as far as your arms will reach over your head.

Position three: Turn your palms out to each side, and with slightly bent elbows, push out with your hands in an arc, bringing your arms back down to your sides with the palms flat against each side of your body.

Repeat this movement at least five times

CHAPTER 27

You're On!
Delivering Your Speech or Story

85

Do not stand up until the person introducing you has finished speaking. Walk to the podium with assurance and anticipation.

86

Before you begin speaking, balance your weight evenly on both feet so that you feel rooted, then gently bend and straighten your knees. This will help you feel centered and to relax your body. Look at your audience. Smile, if doing so feels appropriate. This transmits that you are poised, confident, and that you care about your listeners.

87

Thank the person who introduced you. You might say something like:

— Thank-you. That sounded like someone I would like to know.

— Thank you. That was the best introduction I have ever had.

— Thank you. I wish I knew that much about all of you.

— Everyone say your name, all together. Good, now we all know each other.

88

After the introduction, do not correct minor
inaccuracies. For example, do not introject, "No, no,
I live near the Natural History Museum, not the Art
Museum." Or, "Actually my middle name is Kathleen,
not Catherine."

89

A key indicator of confidence, as well as an easy way to
connect with your audience, is through eye contact. This
does not mean sweeping your eyes over the audience
in a fleeting overview, or swinging your head from
side to side without focusing on individual faces. Look
directly into the eyes of individual audience members
as you make a point. The people with whom you make
genuine eye contact are likely to be the ones who will
come up afterward to compliment you. If you know

that an intimidating person is in the audience, or if you especially want to address a particular individual, with your colored highlighter mark places in your script to search that person out for direct eye contact. If you are shy, look at a specific person's forehead or ear. It will still seem as though you are making direct eye contact.

90

Remember, people listen differently. Just because someone is not making eye contact with you, or appears not to be paying attention, it does not mean that the person is not listening. Don't take it personally. The individual may be jotting down notes or trying to remember a clever turn of a phrase you just used.

I once saw a man in an audience repeatedly glancing at his watch and was convinced that he was bored. Afterward, to my surprise, he expressed sincere enthusiasm, and asked the speaker to visit his Rotary club! He was probably just one of those people who like to consult their watch. Similarly, my husband frequently listens with a concentrated frown on his face. For many years, I thought he did not like what I was saying or how I looked. Then I saw him listening to other speakers with the same concentrated frown!

91

Many speakers tend to talk faster when they sense that they are losing the audience's attention. Perhaps they are hoping to end the speech or story as quickly as possible. Don't do this! Instead, slow down or pause. You will find that this pulls the focus of the audience's attention back to you. When you feel that you have regained the audience's attention, resume your normal pace.

92

Ask a friend or one of the organizers to help with any disruptions that might occur during your talk, such as a malfunctioning microphone, a parent who does not leave with a crying baby, or audience members conversing loudly.

CHAPTER 28

Things to Avoid

93

Try to avoid doing anything that will turn off your audience. This includes:

- ～ Sing-song delivery, narcissistic or distracting information.
- ～ Offensive remarks about physical appearances. Someone who is bald, for example, may not be amused by an anecdote about a bald man and a billiard ball.
- ～ Derogatory ethnic humor.
- ～ Offensive language.
- ～ Using foreign language inserts without translations. Some members of your audience may not know what *que sera sera* means and become distracted or annoyed.

— Self put-downs or excuses: "I was on a trip and did not have time to prepare for this talk the way I had intended to."

— Putting down your audience: "Usually I address politicians, but it is good to be here for your little group."

— Phoniness: "And in conclusion, I want to tell you how nice it was to get to know you." (With thanks to Joyce Saltman for her entertaining workshop: How Not to Give a Talk—The Perils of Humorous and Humorless Presentations at the 1999 Conference of the International Society for Humor Studies. June, 1999, Oakland, California.)

CHAPTER 29

After Your Speech or Story

94

Do not walk off the stage until the applause ends. The manner in which you leave the podium is part of your performance. Leaving too quickly denigrates your talk and gives the impression that you are feeling, "Whew, thank goodness that's over!"

95

When the applause has died down, you can add additional commentary—a brief tag may even merit a second round of applause (double applause.) An interesting phenomenon is that audiences usually applaud louder and longer the second time. You may walk back to your seat during this second applause.

Examples:

"The quote which I used to open this talk with was one of Eleanor Roosevelt's favorite sayings."

"I was especially delighted to be invited to speak to the Sierra Club today, as my son is a newly elected state board member in Oklahoma."

96

Have your business card, flyer, or brochure that includes information on how you can be contacted, available for people to pick up after your presentation.

97

Send a thank-you note to the organization or people who invited you to speak. If you know who recommended you, send them a thank you note as well. Besides being the courteous thing to do, these notes are often read at business meetings and will remind members of your presentation and encourage them to pass along your name to other organizations which engage speakers.

CHAPTER 30
Audience Questions

98

If a question-and-answer period follows your talk, establish guidelines. These might include,

- ∼ "Please, state your name before asking a question."
- ∼ "Please step up to the microphone so that everyone can hear the questions."
- ∼ "We will have fifteen minutes for questions."
- ∼ "We have time for three more questions."

It is a good idea to ask people to use the microphone so that everyone hears their questions. If this is not practical, repeat the question so that everyone knows what you are answering.

The late novelist and "merry prankster" Ken Kesey, used a fabric beach ball with a microphone embedded inside. He tossed this colorful ball to the person who wanted to ask a question and afterward had it tossed back to him.

CHAPTER 31

Contracts

100

If you are a paid speaker, be specific about contracts and money in advance.

Decide whether you want to specify in the contract:

- ~ If you want a percentage of your fee paid in advance.
- ~ What will happen if the event is canceled (you may have declined other lucrative speaking assignments for that date.)
- ~ What provision you will make if you have an emergency and are unable to fulfill the obligation.

Example:
An expensive speaker from out of state arrived on the day of a major snowstorm in the South, and the event was canceled. He had already flown to the location,

had booked a hotel, and was counting on that fee. His contract specified full payment regardless of the turnout.

101

Last but not least, take time after each talk to analyze the experience. Be honest in your self-appraisal, but don't be too hard on yourself, especially at first. Make a list of what you felt was especially successful and then think about the things you would like to improve. Remember, we learn from our mistakes.

> A king asked his wise men
> to bring him something that
> would have the power to
> make him happy when he
> was sad and humble when he
> was exultant. His wise men
> designed a ring inscribed
> with these words:
> *This too shall pass.*
> —Sufi tale

CHAPTER 32

Keynoting

What is a keynote?

The opening talk for a conference that can create the foundation and focus for the entire day, weekend, or week of workshops, discussions and presentations. When you are lucky enough to receive this invitation, you hope to be entertaining, insightful, and inspirational. It is not uncommon for a pithy saying of the keynote speaker to be repeatedly quoted throughout the conference.

Presenting yourself as a specialist

Although you may not be an authority in the area of expertise for the conference you have been invited to open, if you can provide your audience with enthralling information relative to their organization or goals you will be a crowd-pleaser. For example, at a conference for children's authors, you might tell them about the first children's book ever published or divulge why Maurice Sendak dressed Mama Bear in a long skirt in *Little Bear*. A reviewer for the *New York Times* puzzled over this. She decided that Sendak wanted to place his bears in the Victorian era when long skirts were worn, and she wrote this in her review. Later, this reviewer took a job as a children's book editor and when she talked to Sendak about another art project she asked him about this. He told her, "I think bears' legs are ugly, and I didn't want to have to draw them." She wrote, "I was astonished at how wrong my guess was. His reason was purely from an artistic point of view. It had nothing to do with a Victorian setting. "

Another approach is to tell an anecdote or folktale that highlights the theme of the conference.

Sharing the spotlight

It has become fashionable for political candidates to introduce a member of the audience and then relate his or her story. They do this because they have found that audiences identify with an average citizen. By presenting their tale of courage or struggles, this casts a favorable spotlight on the candidate.

Example: Candidate at a political rally:

"Albert Jones from Madison, Wisconsin, found a garbage bag filled with one hundred dollar bills. He works at a Papa John's pizza parlor, has a mortgage, and two children in college. No one is around. No one would ever know. What would you do if you found this? I know many of you would do what Albert did. He posted a sign saying he had found a garbage bag, and if someone could identify the contents he would return it. It was claimed. The owner rewarded Albert, thank goodness, but that's not really my point. Oh, I know, it may seem funny to some of you for a politician to tout honesty. But, *honestly*, folks, if we are going to get our city back on track, we have to be honest about scrutinizing where each candidate's campaign fund is coming from."

I have also found that anecdotes about people in the organization you are addressing are a crowd-pleaser. You may be lucky in pre-conference discussions with the person who invited you to obtain spot-on information that will enhance your talk.

Conversely, it is distracting to name-drop people that are unfamiliar to your audience. You cannot assume that a well-known person in a specific specialty is recognizable to your audience. For all they know, it could be your next-door neighbor. Speaking to a college poetry conference, for example, telling about Ken Kesey regretting that his second novel did not receive the editorial review he was expecting from his publisher is information that is enhanced by identifying his two novels, telling them that one was made into a movie, and the awards it received.

Use of a repeated phrase to structure your talk

A rousing technique in keynotes is to include a story

or anecdote with a refrain that you use repeatedly for emphasis in your talk. The first time you use this phrase you say it. The next time invite the audience to finish it. Just pausing and holding your arms outstretched in an invitational manner will encourage their participation. The third time, just smile and open your arms! Keep in mind that your smiling will elicit audience smiles!

Example: Addressing an audience of Toastmasters

One winter, in a small Eskimo village, I met a little girl, Alice. She told me that when she was four years old, her father took her fishing. He would pull in his line and give his catch to her with instructions to put the fish in a bucket. Alice felt sorry for the fish so she would walk upstream and drop it back in the water. At the end of the day her father had caught ten fish, but when he looked in the bucket, it was empty. He told folks, "I probably caught the same fish ten times." As a result of this experience, Alice's family acquired an expression they used when someone was about to discard an idea or object that might be useful: "Don't Alice it."

Throughout the rest of the speech, the phrase "Don't Alice it" is used to punctuate salient points.

Sharing your work with a wider audience

This brings up the issue of video recording. I find it challenging to interact with a live audience and at the same time create a successful video. Recorded speeches are persuasive when the speaker is looking directly into the camera (communicating with the viewer) and less effective when the viewer is merely observing the presentation. If you have agreed to have your speech videotaped request that the camera crew intersperse shots of the audience and occasionally look directly at the camera so the viewer feels included in that audience. If you are recording a speech for Skype or the Internet, find out from the camera person where to focus your eyes so that you give the impression that you are speaking directly to your remote audience.

Frequently keynote speakers are asked for copies of their talk and/or permission to include it in a publication. As your speech was presented in oral language, I recommend that if this is agreeable, you look over the manuscript before submitting it to make sure it has been translated to literary language. Include a photograph, brief biography, and contact information

CHAPTER 33
Sources for Mini-Stories

There was once a famous Rabbi who always knew the perfect story no matter what point he wanted to make. One day someone asked the Rabbi, "How is it that you always seem to know an appropriate story?"

The Rabbi smiled. "Ah, that reminds me of a story," And he told this tale:

There was once a rich nobleman in Russia who was known far and wide for his great skill in musketry. One day he arrived in a small village and saw a barn covered with bulls-eyes. And, in the center of each bull's-eye there was a bullet hole!

"Who is the marksman?" he asked. To his astonishment, a small boy stepped forward. "Will you show me how you did that?" The boy nodded, and lifting his gun, he aimed at the barn. The bullet hit the barn wall and the boy quickly ran over and drew a series of concentric circles around it so that the bullet hole was in the bull's-eye. "That's how I do it, sir," the boy explained. "I aim for the barn, and then I go over and draw a bull's eye around it."

"You see," the Rabbi explained, "I know a lot of stories. When a question or problem arises, I draw a story around it.

—Adapted from A *Treasury of Jewish Folklore* by Nathan Ausubel, 1948.

∞∞∞

A friend told me another story with a slightly different approach to hitting the bulls-eye, and I like it too.

The Zen master told the people in the fishing town that it was not so difficult to always hit a bull's eye. "Ha," the people said, "show us." The Zen master led the people to a sea cliff. Then he shot his arrow down into the water. "Bull's eye!" he exclaimed.

RECOMMENDED READING

Aesop's Fables. New York: Grosset & Dunlap, 1848.

Ausubel, Nathan. *A Treasury of Jewish Folklore.* New York: Crown Publishers, 1948.

∞∞∞

The following books are all collections of "Urban Legends" from folklorist, Jan Harold Brunvand.

The Vanishing Hitchhiker. New York: Norton & Co., 1981.

The Choking Doberman. New York: Norton & Co., 1984.

The Mexican Pet. New York: Norton & Co., 1986.

Curses! Broiled Again! (New York: Norton & Co., 1989.

The Baby Train (New York: Norton & Co., 1993.

∞∞∞

Creeden, Sharon. *Fair is Fair.* Little Rock, Arkansas: August House, 1994.

_____. *In Full Bloom: Tales of Women in Their Prime.* Little Rock, Arkansas: August House, 1999.

∞∞∞

de Mello, Anthony. *One Minute Wisdom.* New York: Doubleday, 1986.

———. *Taking Flight: A Book of Story Meditations.* New York: Doubleday, 1988.

———. *The Heart of the Enlightened.* New York: Doubleday, 1989.

ooooo

deVos, Gail. *Storytelling for Young Adults.* Westport, CT: Libraries Unlimited, 2003.
Includes an annotated bibliography listing hundreds of story sources.

Ellis, Elizabeth. *From Plot to Narrative.* Little Rock: Parkhurst Brothers, 2012

Feldman, Christina and Jack Kornfield. *Stories of the , Stories of the Heart: Parables of the Spiritual Path from Around the World.* San Francisco: Harper, 1991.

Fish, Robert. *The Woman Who Walked to Paradise: Stories for Coping in a Chaotic World.* San Jose, CA: Fish Tales Press, 2000.

Ford, Linda M. *Musings: Tales of Truth & Wisdom.* Golden, CO: Fulcrum Resources, 2000.

Forest, Heather. *Wisdom Tales from Around the World.* Little Rock, AR: August House, 1996.

Funk, Wilfred. *Word Origins and their Romantic Stories.* New York: Grosset & Dunlap, 1950.

Funk, Charles E. *Thereby Hangs a Tale: Stories of Curious Word Origins.* New York: Warner Library, 1972.

∞∞∞

Haven, Ken. *Marvels of Science: 50 Fascinating 5-Minute Reads.* Englewood, Colorado: Libraries Unlimited, 1994.

———. *Amazing American Women: 40 Fascinating 5-Minute Reads.* Englewood, Colorado: Libraries Unlimited, 1995.

———. *Marvels of Math: Fascinating Reads and Awesome Activities.* Englewood, Colorado: Libraries Unlimited, 1996.

∞∞∞

Kaye, Danny. *Around the World Story Book.* New York: Random House, 1960.

Jaffe, Nina and Steve Zeitlin. *While Standing on one Foot: Puzzle Stories and Wisdom Tales from the Jewish Tradition.* New York: Henry Holt & Co., 1993.

Jones, Charlotte Foltz. *Mistakes that Worked.* New York: Doubleday, 1991.

∞∞∞

Kelsey, Alice Geer. *Once the Hodja.* New York: Longmans, Green, 1943

———. *Once the Mullah: Persian Folk Tales.* New York: Longmans, Green & Co., 1954.

∞∞∞

MacDonald. Margaret Read. *The Storyteller's Sourcebook: A Subject, Title and Motif Index to Folklore Collections for Children.* Detroit, MI : Neal-Schuman Publishers in association with Gale Research, 1982.
Most children's librarians have a non-circulating copy of this book that you can use in the library.

———. *Peace Tales: World Folktales to Talk About.* Hamden, CT: Linnet Books, 1992.

∞∞∞

Mendoza, Patrick M. *Extraordinary People in Extraordinary Times: Heroes, Sheroes and Villains.* Englewood, CO: Libraries Unlimited, 1999.

Nahmad, H. M. *The Peasant and the Donkey: Tales of the Near and Middle East.* New York: Henry Z. Walck, 1968.

Nelson, Pat. *Magic Minutes: Quick Read-Alouds for Every Day.* Englewood, CO: Libraries Unlimited, 1993.

Niemi, Loren. *The New Book of Plots.* Little Rock: Parkhurst Brothers, 2012

Reps, Paul. *Zen Flesh, Zen Bones: A Collection of Zen and Pre-Zen Writings.* Tokyo, Rutland, VT: C.E. Tuttle Co., 1957.

∞∞∞

Shah, Indries. *Wisdom of the Idiots.* London: Octagon Press, 1969.

———. *Tales of the Dervishes.* New York: Dutton, 1970.

———. *The Way of the Sufi.* New York: Dutton, 1970.

∞∞∞

Shenkman, Richard and Kurt Reiger. *One-Night Stands with American History: Amusing and Little-Known Incidents.* New York : Morrow, 1980.

Sutherland, James. *The Oxford Book of Literary Anecdotes* Oxford: Clarendon Press, 1975.

Tolstoy, Leo. *Fables and Fairy Tales.* New York: New American Library, 1962.

Walker, Barbara. *Watermelons, Walnuts and the Wisdom of Allah, and Other Tales of the Hodja* (New York: Parents' Magazine Press, 1967.

∞∞∞

See also:

Cordry, Harold V. *The Multicultural Dictionary of Proverbs,* Jefferson, N.C.: McFarland, 1997.

Varasdi, J. Allen. *Myth Information: More than 500 Popular Misconceptions, Fallacies and Misbeliefs Explained.* New York: Ballantine Books, 1989.

Wilder, Lilyan. *7 Steps to Fearless Speaking.* New York: J. Wiley, 1999.

From *Aesop's Fables*. New York: Grosset & Dunlap, 1848.

**If you would like to know more about Ruth Stotter
and/or storytelling, please visit:**

**www.storynet.org
www.parkhustbrothers.com**

RUTH STOTTER, M.A. directed the Dominican University (San Rafael, California) Storytelling program for fourteen years. She is a program, seminar, and workshop leader and performer on five continents. Former chairperson of the Aesop Committee for the American Folklore Society, Stotter has also hosted and produced storytelling radio programs. Interested in Jungian psychology and analyzing stories, she incorporates origami, puppetry and string stories into performances. Listed in Who's Who in the World, Stotter is a recipient of the Oracle Lifetime Achievement in Storytelling from the National Storytelling Network (USA).

NOTES

NOTES